YOUR
RECORD
BOOK

forget about babies and bathwater,
this one's for mum

ANNA CROSBIE

Summersdale Publishers Ltd
46 West Street
Chichester
West Sussex
PO19 IRP
United Kingdom

www.summersdale.com

ISBN: 1 84024 278 7

Mum's Name

....

Baby's Name

....

Baby Born On

....

·Contents·

notes·thoughts·photos·mementoes

notes·thoughts·photos·mementoes

A Message to Baby About The Birth

overall, your birth was...

....

....

....

names I called your Dad

....

....

....

things I said to others in the room

....

....

....

the best bit

....

....

....

the worst bit

....

....

....

the funniest or most emotional bit

....

....

....

Bringing Baby Home

I was most nervous about

....
....
....

things Dad did to help

....
....
....

some presents I got

....
....
....

some presents Baby got

....
....
....

memorable first achievements

....
....
....

memorable first disasters

....
....
....

notes·thoughts·photos·mementoes

notes·thoughts·photos·mementoes

Hey! I'm Not Pregnant!

Before you forget, note all those things you meant to
record in some sort of pregnancy journal.
(You know, the journal you never got around to starting...)

the best things about *not being* pregnant

....
....
....

what I did when I found out I was pregnant

....
....
....

the stage of pregnancy I most enjoyed

....
....
....

the stage of pregnancy I least enjoyed

....
....
....

what I miss most about being pregnant

....
....
....

other memories or whinges about pregnancy

....
....
....

My Poor Body

The whole world will be showing an interest in your newborn baby; how big she's grown or how his hair's changing colour. Meanwhile, you and your body are embarking on a **monstrous** recovery process and it can feel like no one is even noticing! It will be of only small consolation, but WE know what you and your body have to endure in your first weeks back home.

Don't suffer in silence – record your discomfort so in years to come you can remember the sympathy you didn't get!

Ailment	Bad	V.V. Bad	Just OK
stitches (ouch!)	❑	❑	❑
constipation	❑	❑	❑
cracked nipples	❑	❑	❑
stretch marks like the Nile Delta	❑	❑	❑
incontinence	❑	❑	❑
mastitis	❑	❑	❑
I'm going bald!	❑	❑	❑
complete figure loss	❑	❑	❑
others...			
....	❑	❑	❑
....	❑	❑	❑
....	❑	❑	❑

Necessary Inspiration Page

(or, when you find motherhood a struggle...daydream!)

things I'm looking forward to when Baby is 1

....
....
....

things I'm looking forward to when Baby is 2

....
....
....

things I'm looking forward to when Baby is a toddler

....
....
....

things I'm looking forward to when Baby is at school

....
....
....

things I'm looking forward to when Baby is a teenager

....
....
....

things I'm looking forward to when Baby is an adult!

....
....
....

things I'll do when I feel fit, slimmer and sexy again...

....
....

Mum's Growth Chart

Use this Chart of Milestones to record your evolution from new mum to Your-Former-Old-Self.

	Date	Evolutionary Confidence Points (ECPs)
First alcoholic binge	....	10
First guilt-free slice of chocolate cake	....	10
First day I bothered to wear make-up	....	10
First day I bothered to style my hair	....	10
First outing without baby (to ....)	....	50
Day breasts fitted favourite (non-maternity) bra	....	50
Day when bum fitted favourite pair of jeans	....	50
First car journey of over two hours with baby	....	100
First CHEER-MYSELF-UP shopping mission (to ....)	....	100
First articulate debate about current affairs	....	150
First felt like a Sexy Woman instead of Frumpy Slob	....	500
First attempt at sex (whether successful or not)	....	1000
First acknowledged that having a gorgeous baby is IMMEASURABLY more important than absolutely anything else anyway	....	5000

evolution complete ☐
date ticked ..../.................../...........

Time-Out-From-Baby Rota

(Copy this for your fridge door immediately!)

	Mon	Tues	Wed	Thur	Fri	Sat	Sun
Mum							
Dad							

How The Rota Works...

1. Each parent is allowed to book four Time-Out-From-Baby Sessions.

2. Each is for a minimum of 1 hour; maximum time by mutual agreement.

3. Each parent may allocate a Time-Out Session for whatever they choose regardless of how trivial it may seem to the other parent. Some examples: swim, game of squash, go for a walk, go to pub, visit a friend, watch favourite tv programme, sit and read Sunday papers, gardening, or just time to soak in a bath uninterrupted.

4. Time-Out Sessions can only be traded by mutual consent.

5. The aim of the game is to give both parents some respite.

6. The real aim of the game is to ensure neither parent feels more cheated of spare time than the other...

notes·thoughts·photos·mementoes

notes·thoughts·photos·mementoes

Therapy for Stressed Mums

(Remember to take time out to enjoy your baby!)

Genetic Stock-Take!

Feature	Dad's or Mum's? Date	Dad's or Mum's? Date	Dad's or Mum's? Date
Head Shape	~	~	~
Ears	~	~	~
Eyes	~	~	~
Nose	~	~	~
Cheeks	~	~	~
Mouth	~	~	~
Smile	~	~	~
Hands	~	~	~
Feet	~	~	~
Hair	~	~	~

Take Baby's Hand and Footprints
Yes it's daft, but they are fun to look back on!

Doom, Gloom & Depression

This page is for your gloomiest moments.
When you feel at breaking-point, try the following:

1. Remember you are NOT abnormal. All parents feel like this from time to time, and if they tell you otherwise they are *without a doubt* lying!

2. If necessary, put your baby in its crib or cot (screaming or not) and walk into another room (or into your garden if you have one); breathe deeply and slowly for ten breaths. As you return inside, remember that the situation is NOT your fault, and, as importantly, it's *not your baby's fault either.*

3. Ring a close friend or relative and unload your stress on them. They will understand, and it is *precisely* at times like this that your close friends and family are your greatest asset. Don't feel a burden – if you think about it, they probably unload their stress on you all the time.

4. Ring your Health Visitor if you are worried about your baby (or yourself). They are remarkable professionals who have seen MILLIONS of New Mums crumple with stress, exhaustion or disillusionment. They won't judge you, they will listen, and – if it's something that concerns you - they won't recall your desperation at a dinner party in five years' time ('Remember when you rang me in tears and said you could ...').

5. If you prefer greater anonymity, phone a national helpline. Numerous organisations exist to help out parents just like you and me. Your local GP or Citizens Advice Bureau should have an up-to-date and local list of useful groups and numbers, but here are two for starters:

- CRY-SIS: help and support for families with excessively crying, sleepless and demanding babies and children:
  ph. 0207 404 5011.
- Parentline: support in times of trouble and stress:
  ph. 0808 8002222.

The Truth About Breast-Feeding

Breast-Feeding:
(Tick if you agree)

- ☐ Is Pants! I didn't bother with it
- ☐ Hurts like hell
- ☐ Is easy! I can breast-feed and iron at the same time!
- ☐ Is sooooooo BORING!
- ☐ Is more fun when done in a public place
- ☐ If Mother Nature had *really* intended us to breast-feed she would have given Mothers a third arm (i.e. extra hand with which to hold the coffee cup)

A Mental Game To Play Whilst Breast-Feeding:
Compose A Limerick About Breasts!

(Some Examples We Knocked Together)
There was a young woman from Devizes
whose breasts were two different sizes
one was so small, it was no use at all
the other was so big it won prizes!

There was a young woman from Frome
whose breasts took up far too much room
they popped out of her shirt, then hung down to her skirt
and had to be hoisted back up with a broom!

There was a young lady from Heywood
whose breasts were no longer any good
whenever she sat, they filled up her whole lap
and sagged right down to her knees when she stood.

Complete your limerick here:
There was a young lady from

....

....

....

....

Losing the Moral High-Ground

Don't despair if you're not living up to your expectations ... You're not alone!

The Theory	The Reality	Done It? ✓
• I'll stop using disposable nappies after the first few months.	'I know, I know, I must, I will... next week.'	☐
• I'll make my own baby food – none of this canned stuff in my house.	'Well I did get as far as buying some new ice-cube trays and a new blender...'	☐
• I won't become a victim of fashion and pay a fortune for cute baby clothes.	'Oh it's gorgeous! I can't afford it but will treat myself just this once.'	☐
• The baby won't rule our lives, we'll *make* the time to maintain a social life and go out, just the two of us.	'Ha! We're too bloody tired to go out, and anyhow, now that we have to budget for childcare we can't afford to go out.'	☐
• I won't let MY baby crawl around with a disgusting snotty nose and spewy bib.	'Oh who cares? Chill out, I'll clean him up in a minute!'	☐
• I'll keep all Baby's toys in discreet storage boxes and *minimise* their visual and physical disruption to the house.	'Plastic rules OK! One must have a disorganised pile of it in every room! If you can't navigate past a few baby gyms then don't bother visiting.'	☐
• I'll take Baby to regular developmental classes: massage, soft play, sound and movement, swimming, weekly health clinic, weekly playgroup, etc.	'It's too cold. It's too hot. I'm too tired. Baby's too tired. There's too much traffic. I'm not sure Baby enjoys them. I just can't be bothered!'	☐
• I won't wear leggings and baggy jumpers post-pregnancy.	'I don't fit many of my *nice* clothes, and any I do I must protect from baby spew.'	☐

The Theory   The Reality   Done It?

                                                        ✓

- If Baby's father is annoying me
  I won't sulk; we'll communicate
  rationally and sort it out.

  'If *he's* behaving like a stubborn,
  spoilt ten-year-old than so will
  bloody I!'   ☐

- I'll open Baby a savings account
  and save regularly.

  'Even if I did have any disposable
  income, my own need to be
  cheered up is far greater.'   ☐

- During my maternity leave
  I'll finally read all those books
  I've bought and left unopened
  on the bookshelf.

  'Read?! It's enough to focus my
  sleep-deprived eyes on the
  formula milk instructions...'   ☐

- I won't talk graphically
  about my labour and
  childbirth at dinner parties.

  'Well she did ask ... and what else
  have I done lately to talk about?'   ☐

- I won't begrudge Baby's
  father the odd hour off so
  he can do his sports
  training and see his mates.

  'Selfish git. There's NO WAY he's
  having more time off from baby
  duties than I do.'   ☐

- I will ALWAYS remember
  that it's more important
  Baby grows up respecting
  me than liking me.

  Mmmmm. No one told me the
  discipline thing would be this hard!
  I'll work on installing respect next
  year, right now it's easier to let
  Baby be Boss.'   ☐

- I won't start watching
  trashy daytime television
  programmes whilst on
  maternity leave.

  'They allow me to sit still and not
  have to think. Go away.'   ☐

- I won't call my baby a
  nonsensical array of
  mushy pet names.

  'Whoops! It just happened!'   ☐

- I won't let Baby get
  used to sleeping in our bed.

  'It's EASIER! Besides, we enjoy
  having him snuggling and snorting
  between us...'   ☐

notes·thoughts·photos·mementoes

notes·thoughts·photos·mementoes

The Childcare Dilemma Doodler

All Mums will agonise over childcare. To go back to work, not to go back
to work? Financial ruin if you don't, emotional torture if you do?
Use this 'dilemma doodler' to note your worries and options.

Consider...	Work Full-time	Work Part-time	Don't Work
for Mum's mental sanity			
against Mum's mental sanity			
for Baby's welfare & development			
against Baby's welfare & development			
for Financial			
against Financial			

The First Christmas

Baby was ____ months old

I felt:

☐ Knackered
☐ Fat
☐ Excited
☐ Proud
☐ Other ....

I:

☐ Spent far too much money on Baby's presents
☐ Was annoyed that Baby got more presents than me
☐ Took an excessive number of photos
☐ Had too many relatives in the house
☐ Other...

where we were

....

who we were with

....
....

the best thing about my first Christmas as a Mum

....
....
....

the worst thing about my first Christmas as a Mum

....
....

notes·thoughts·photos·mementoes

notes·thoughts·photos·mementoes

The First Holiday

Hint: for a happy holiday with Baby...

1. Lower your expectations
2. Be grateful for small successes along the way
3. Plan daily activities with military precision around Baby's feed and sleep times – especially car journeys and trips to public places
4. If you are easily stressed, go on holiday to somewhere familiar, where you know the whereabouts of:
   - The nearest public toilet
   - The nearest car park
   - The nearest shelter (from sun, wind, rain, crowds, noise, depending on Baby's mood)
   - The nearest baby-friendly shop (for coffee and/or chocolate therapy)
5. Always anticipate Baby's boredom and have antidotes to hand

where we went

....

....

things that went wrong

....

....

things that went right!

....

....

level of respite Mum achieved:

☐ Fantastic – even managed to *relax!*

☐ Pretty good – slightly less exhausting than being at home

☐ OK – still exhausted but a change of scenery was terrific

☐ Forget it – next time I'm going on holiday alone!

notes·thoughts·photos·mementoes

notes·thoughts·photos·mementoes

The First Birthday

Baby's First Birthday should actually be a celebration dedicated to the parents, called something like Thank-God-We-Survived-Day, or Thank-God-It's-Not-This-Time-Last-Year-Day.

So have a quiet celebration of your own!

treats I bought myself

....
....
....

some poignant thoughts about the past year

....
....
....

how we celebrated

....
....
....
....
....
....

who with?

....
....
....

Present Tally
Mum_____ Baby_____
(Humph! Guessed as much!)

A Photo of Me, One Year On
(make it a glamorous one!)

A Photo of Baby, One Year On

Baby's Changing Temperament

Motherhood is a daily game of
'Guess-What-Mood-Baby-Will-Be-In-Today'.
Play this game with Dad to solve housework disputes,
or with some other Mum friends (loser pays for the wine)...

☹ →	Baby falls asleep in buggy Advance 3	😐	Baby suffers Supermarket RAGE Back 5	🙂	YOU WIN! For Now
Baby plays with new baby-gym Advance 3	☹	Baby doesn't give a damn: Miss a turn	😐	Baby woken up by its enormous poo Back 3	😄 ←
☹ →	Baby ignores cat today Advance 3	🙂	Baby loves baby-rice meal today Advance 3	😐	Baby will NOT lie still for new nappy Back 5
Baby's juice cup is ONLY for throwing Back 3	😐	Baby will NOT sit on Mum's lap Back 3	🙂	Baby HATES bath time Miss a turn	☹ ←
😐 →	Baby lies still for new nappy Advance 5	☹	Baby behaves at shops Advance 3	😐	Baby sits happily in high-chair Advance 3
Baby thinks car seat is a MONSTER Back 3	☹	Baby enjoys bath time Advance 1	🙂	Baby happy in car seat Advance 5	😐 ←
Start (Roll dice) →	Baby likes being dressed Advance 3	☹	Baby HATES being dressed Back 3	😐	'WAAAAGH! Go away! I want my DAD! WAAAAGH!' Back 3

An Emotional Cocktail

Just like Baby, Mums are entitled to changing temperaments. The fact is, you experience an exhausting and bewildering array of emotions, like you've probably never experienced before, in the course of each day. Research has shown that new Dads benefit from some forewarning as to what mood Mum is in at the time he opens the front door every evening. (Wise Dads know it will definitely have changed from the mood you were in on the telephone an hour earlier.) Help out by posting this mood barometer on the wall, just inside the door ...

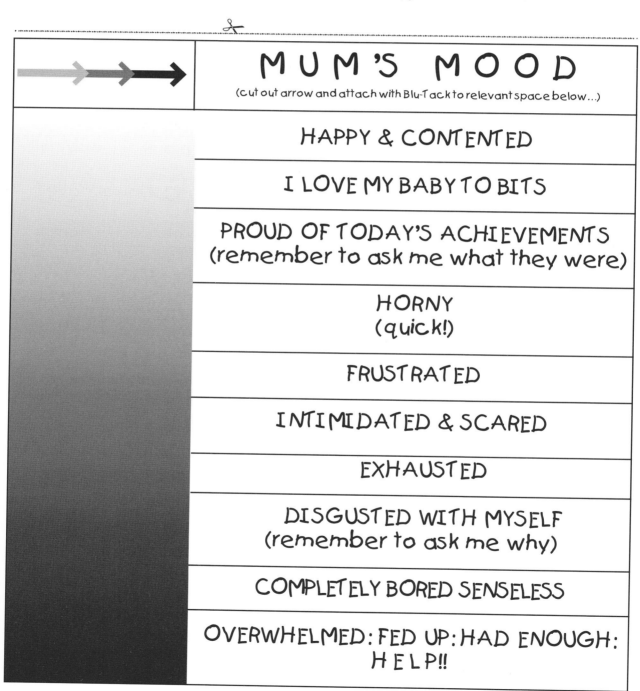

MUM'S MOOD

(cut out arrow and attach with Blu-Tack to relevant space below...)

HAPPY & CONTENTED

I LOVE MY BABY TO BITS

PROUD OF TODAY'S ACHIEVEMENTS
(remember to ask me what they were)

HORNY
(quick!)

FRUSTRATED

INTIMIDATED & SCARED

EXHAUSTED

DISGUSTED WITH MYSELF
(remember to ask me why)

COMPLETELY BORED SENSELESS

OVERWHELMED: FED UP: HAD ENOUGH: HELP!!

The Baby-Gym Break

A Baby-Gym Break officially starts when you place Baby on its playmat, beneath its Baby-Gym. It officially ends when Baby gets fed up with the stimuli dangling above its head, and starts to cry. Average Baby-Gym Breaks last twenty minutes, but have been known to last up to forty minutes in exceptional cases.

A Baby-Gym Break is a time management phenomenon! New Mums can achieve more in a mere Baby-Gym Break than they used to achieve in a whole morning. There is one Golden Rule to the correct use of a Baby-Gym Break:

NEVER USE IT TO DO HOUSEWORK.

Instead, try some of the following:
Lie on sofa with legs up and eyes closed
Walk around your garden if you have one
Phone a friend
Make a cup of coffee and read a newspaper, magazine or novel
Have a bath and shave your legs
Have a shower and wash, dry and *style* your hair
Put on some make-up as a treat
Bake some muffins or your favourite cake

Or, do a Baby-Gym Break work-out of your own:
(wait for your 6-week doctor's check first!)

1. 30 sit ups
2. 30 press ups
3. 30 side stretches
   (Reach arm over head and lean and stretch)
4. 30 squats
   (Stand with knees over toes, squat up and down slowly)
5. 30 knee raises
   (Bring alternate knees up to chest, with back straight. Bring opposite elbow down to meet knee)
6. 30 toe kicks
   (Stand with hands on shoulders. Raise alternate legs as high as you can and kick feet in front of you. Reach forward with opposite hand and touch your toes, if you can)
7. 30 lunges
   (Stand with hands on hips, step forward and lower alternate knees to the floor)

Housework

Housework is simply *not* a priority when you're a New Mum!
Try adopting the following principles to alleviate housework arguments.

Housework Mum will TRY to do during the day (if Baby allows)
= the emptying and loading jobs:
dishwasher, washing machine, dryer, rubbish bins.

Housework to be SHARED by Mum and Partner (during evenings and weekends)
Vacuuming, cleaning bathroom, ironing, dusting,
putting things away and general de-cluttering.

Or sit down with your Husband or Partner and discuss your own divisions of responsibility
(it may seem trivial but housework is a major cause of arguments in households with new babies!)

Mum	Dad
....	....
....	....
....	....
....	....
....	....
....	....
....	....
....	....
....	....
....	....
....	....
....	....

Mum's Soap Box Corner

As Baby grows older, the more confident you'll become at voicing your dissatisfaction with society's *frequent* disregard for Mums and babies.

What disregard for Mums and babies? Well! *For example...*

- Inadequate provision of paid maternity and paternity leave
- Why most professional career ladders *still* can't accommodate part-time work or job sharing
- Why the cost of child-care *still* isn't tax deductible
- Why dry-cleaners don't offer bulk discount rates for baby sick
- Why scientists have discovered a cure for washing machine lint but not for morning sickness
- Illegal parking in 'family and child' spaces at the supermarket
- The cost of toddlers' shoes and maternity bras
- The demise of courteous gentlemen who help carry buggies up stairs at train stations
- Those cafés and restaurants that *still* don't provide high-chairs
- How airlines can charge what they do for 2-year-old passengers
- Non-parents (who have yet to change a nappy) lecturing you about your irresponsible use of disposables

You will soon develop some pet issues of your own – things that **really get your goat**. Record them here, and see if society has advanced by the time your daughter becomes a New Mum herself ...

....

....

....

....

....

....

....

I'm A Mum and I'll Be as Stroppy as I Damned Well Want!

Record your evolving confidence to publicly state an opinion, disagree, or even make a complete ass of yourself, all in the name of your baby.

first dispute regarding public transport

....

first disagreement with a shop assistant/waiter/waitress

....

first argument with a civil servant or official

....

first blazing row with ignorant male about baby-related issue

....

first wanted to wee on someone's floor
when they told you there was no public toilet or baby
changing room for you to use

....

best all-time display

....

worst all-time display

....

Do They Think Us Mums Are Stupid?

To ensure you won't be so easily conned next time, make a list of all the things clever marketing convinced you to purchase for you or Baby that turned out to be *utterly useless.*

For example!

Stretch-mark prevention and repair creams

Breast pumps

Leaky breast pads

Any magazine with the words 'Regain Your Figure in Just Six Weeks' on the cover

Your List of Complete-Waste-of-Money Items:

....

....

....

....

....

....

....

....

....

....

....

....

....

....

....

....

....

....

The Martyr Mummy Game

New Mums inevitably end up talking about the horrors of childbirth and trials of Motherhood at dinner parties. We are blameless – of course – it is the fault of something that remains surging through our hormones. (The clinical term is *Martyr-Mummy-itis.*) Refine your tactics now, ready for your next dinner party.

Stage I: Labour Martyrdom

Martyr Mummy Points Tally	Martyr Mummy Points Value
☐ Labour less than 10 hours	5
☐ Labour 10-20 hours	10
☐ Labour 20-30 hours	20
☐ Labour 30 hours or more	100
☐ Emergency Caesarean	50
☐ Elective Caesarean	5
☐ No episiotomy/stitches	5
☐ 5-10 stitches	20
☐ More than 10 stitches	30
☐ Complete loss of perineum	50
☐ Pooed during labour (embarrassment bonus points)	50
☐ Vomited during labour	10
☐ Ambulance journey during labour	50
☐ Happy Epidural experience	0
☐ Horrendous Epidural experience	50
☐ Forceps delivery	50
☐ Ventouse delivery	50
☐ Planned birth at home	20
☐ Unplanned birth at home	50
☐ Waterbirth	20
☐ Unplanned birth in car or public place	50
☐ Waters broke in public place (weeeeeeeeeee!)	50
☐ Made Husband/Partner faint (what a wimp, poor you!)	50

The Martyr Mummy Game: Stage II

How did you fare in the Labour stage of the game?
Record your Stage I point tally here: _____

Stage II: Coping With Baby Martyrdom

Martyr Mummy Points Tally	Martyr Mummy Points Value
❏ No nurse/nanny/nearby family member/friend to help out	20
❏ Baby slept through the night before it was six weeks old	deduct 100
❏ Prolonged cracked nipples and/or mastitis	20
❏ Number of toddlers aged four or under also in your care	10 each

Things you did in desperation to get baby to sleep:

❏ Drove baby around block in pyjamas at 3 a.m.	10
❏ Played it a tape of whale or dolphin music, or womb sounds	10
❏ Pushed Baby to and fro in buggy for an hour or more	10

Things you did before Baby turned 6 months old:

❏ Went on a long-haul flight between 10-20 hours	20
❏ Went on long-haul flight over 20 hours (are you mad?)	100
❏ Moved house	100
❏ Drove through Europe in a camper-van (yes, this happens!)	100
❏ Split up with Husband or Partner (sadly, this happens too)	500
❏ Got pregnant again (planned)	50
❏ Got pregnant again (unplanned)	100
❏ Got back to your pre-pregnancy weight (cow!)	deduct 50
❏ Went back to work part-time	100
❏ Went back to work full-time	200

Record your Stage II points tally here: _____

Total Martyr Mummy Points: ____ 🏆

notes·thoughts·photos·mementoes

notes·thoughts·photos·mementoes

How Am I ?!!

Sometimes, the most irritating thing you can ask a New Mum is 'How are you coping?' or 'Are you enjoying Motherhood?' Because, the truth is, most New Mums can't actually make up their minds. To help any irritating people understand why you can't make up your mind, show them this handy diagram of your brain and say

'How the Hell would you feel?'

Fill in the gaps with your own **most prevalent thoughts**,
if you can make up your mind ...

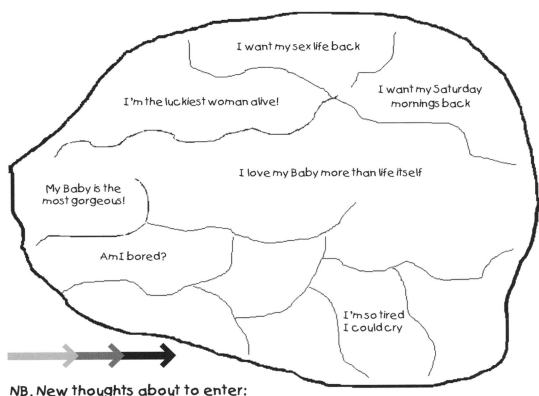

I want my sex life back

I want my Saturday mornings back

I'm the luckiest woman alive!

I love my Baby more than life itself

My Baby is the most gorgeous!

Am I bored?

I'm so tired I could cry

NB. New thoughts about to enter:
What's for dinner?
Do you need a new nappy my schnoodlekims?
Why am I so bloody fat?

A Psychosocioblabalogical Assessment

To make sure you're keeping things in perspective and have some semblance of sane priorities, take this useful little test:

1. Rank these things in order of your Love:
    - ❑ Favourite slothy cardigan
    - ❑ Credit card
    - ❑ Chocolate
    - ❑ Willies
    - ❑ Very, very, very expensive lipstick
    - ❑ Baby
    - ❑ Full body massage

2. Choose two only. 'My Love for Baby is ...'
    - ❑ All-consuming
    - ❑ Eternal
    - ❑ Exhausting
    - ❑ Rewarding beyond measure
    - ❑ Unconditional
    - ❑ Scary
    - ❑ ....

3. Fill in the pie graph
How much time this week did you spend on?

Colour code
a) Baby ❑
b) Shopping & housework ❑
c) Nurturing your relationship
   with Daddy ❑
d) Work ❑
e) You! ❑

Reputation Preservation Graphs

Amount of adult conversation you can hold *before* mentioning Baby

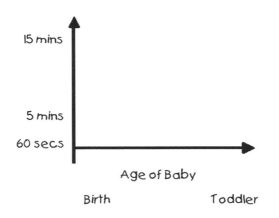

The 'She Can't Talk About Anything Else' Curve

Time spent perfecting your hair, outfit, accessories and make-up before going out in public

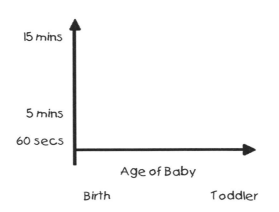

The 'How A Total Stranger Perceives You' Curve

What Do *Your* Graphs Look Like?

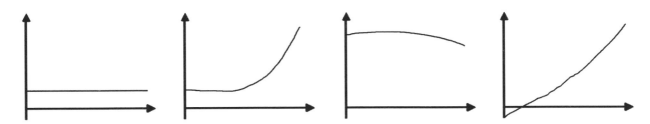

And what do the graphs mean? Are you *Mrs About Average*? Are you *Mrs Hardened Career Mummy*? Are you *Mrs Boring*? Or are you *Mrs Let Herself Go*?

We have no idea! You have to analyse the answer to that one yourself!

Planning the Next Baby? Consider...

Now you've got some baby experience, the planning of your next baby will probably be very different from your first. Here are some typical examples of the comments overheard at playgroups and dinner parties:

- 'We're going to start trying for our next baby the day our first learns to walk.'

- 'I will <u>never</u> be heavily pregnant through the height of summer again and I don't care about anything else.'

- 'No one told us about planning birthdays in relation to the start of the school year (September). Our next will be born in July or August so it can start school as soon as possible after turning four.'

- 'Having my maternity leave during the bleak winter was a complete waste; I didn't get any gardening done.'

- 'I want their birthdays spread throughout the calendar year – it's easier to manage the cost of birthday presents and parties.'

- 'We need to have our second baby as soon as possible so we can secure a place with our absolutely brilliant child-minder.'

- 'Apparently sibling rivalry is less if the age gap is minimal.'

- 'There's no point in salvaging my former body until the next baby is done –asap!'

- 'We won't even consider our next baby until this baby is fully potty trained.'

- 'We planned our first so meticulously, the next one we're just going to have lots of sex and see what happens!'

- 'We want the children grown up and out of the house by the time we turn fifty, so we'll have to have our babies fairly close together – pain now for peace later!'

And If You Think Babies Are Hard Work ...

FACT:
The stage of parenting you are living through is ALWAYS succeeded by an infinitely worse stage of parenting.

THE MORAL OF THE STORY:
Enjoy your baby while it's still a baby, because soon it will be a ...TODDLER!

Example 1: Enjoy your baby while it's a mere stationary blob:
Once it starts to crawl you will anguish constantly over the potential hazards of electrical sockets and cords, dropped coins, and dog poo.

Example 2: Enjoy your baby while it still can't talk:
Once it talks it will be capable of answering back, or bombarding you with an exhausting repetition of 'DOWN!' 'UP!' 'WHY?' 'MORE!' 'JUUUUUIICE!' 'Want THAT!' 'MINE!' but mainly, just 'NO!'

Example 3: Babies have less capacity to humiliate you
A six-week-old baby, screaming blue murder at 4 a.m. is undoubtedly hard work. But (and this is meant to cheer you up ... honest) compared to your happy two-year-old toddler undergoing a sudden personality change, and throwing himself onto the café floor (because you cut his sandwich into *squares* instead of triangles), believe me, your six-week-old is an angel!

Example 4: Your baby doesn't belong to the Manners Police
Your baby loves you unconditionally. You are its idol, its hero (its provider of milk). Alas, when your baby becomes a toddler you will be *judged*, and can no longer do any of the following in its presence: fart, pick your nose, eat the last piece of chocolate, have sex, slag off your neighbours or relatives, or stand by the fridge door and drink orange juice from the carton.

Example 5: You don't have to exaggerate just to protect your baby
When your toddler asks you 'Why can't I walk on the road?' you have to reply 'Because a car might come along and squash you and you will die,' and this makes you feel REALLY lousy. (NB. You also have to emphasise the dangers of fire, drowning, and strangers, and what too much sugar does to teeth. It's awful.)

Feel Like a Laugh?

Remember the earlier Losing The Moral High-Ground pages? Well, set yourself some Theory V. Reality targets for toddler parenting. Revisit them in a few years, and we *guarantee you'll be disappointed!*

....
....
....
....
....
....
....
....
....
....
....
....
....
....
....
....
....
....
....
....
....
....
....
....

The Little Joys of Motherhood

- Browsing in toy shops (and taking a whole hour to spend the few coins in your pocket)
- When your walking one-year-old first slips their little hand in yours
- Christmas, Easter and Birthdays
- Leaning on the cot edge for ten minutes just to watch Baby sleep
- Choosing between Tigger napkins or Goofy paper cups
- Baby's first train set ('No, no, watch *Mummy do it!*')
- Making ticklish Baby laugh
- Playing 'peek-a-boo'
- Slurping, grunting, breast-feeding Baby
- The 'I can crawl fast, giggle and squeal *all at once*' Baby
- Happy, splashy Baby in the bath
- Carrying already asleep Baby upstairs to bed

My Favourite Little Joys of Motherhood (lest I forget...)

....

....

....

....

....

....

....

....

....

....

....

....

....

....

....

U.O.Me

Dear [_____] *enter Baby's name here*

The following is a true and accurate record of all items that comprise the total cumulative value that shall be deducted from your pocket money allowance, whence you begin demanding it in the future.

This U.O.Me adheres to the Child and Parenting Contract to which you signed up on the day of your birth (the contract signed duly on your behalf by your Father), and represents the fair recompense that I, your Mother, rightly deserve for all breakages and losses incurred during the course of your upbringing.

Yours ever,

[_____] *enter your name here*

Item	Value (£)	Occurrence
(examples)		
Ceramic vase	£50	broken when you climbed shelves
Cashmere jumper	£42	ruined by your vomit

....

....

....

....

....

....

....

....

....

....

Cumulative Value _____   Dated __/__/__

Babies & Sexlessness

Sexlessness *n.* the state of having no sex.
Sexless *adj.* lacking in sexual interest,
attractiveness or activity.

Consider this Catatonic Irony:

Sex creates Babies, but Babies create Sexlessness.

The graphical representation of a typical sex life follows:

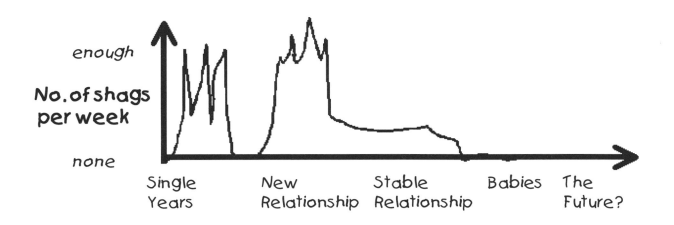

Note the demise of sexual activity from the heights of
The New Relationship Shagfest
to the futile lows of
Post-Baby Sexlessness

Predict Your Future Sexlessness

(fill in the graphs as they might apply to YOUR sexlife)

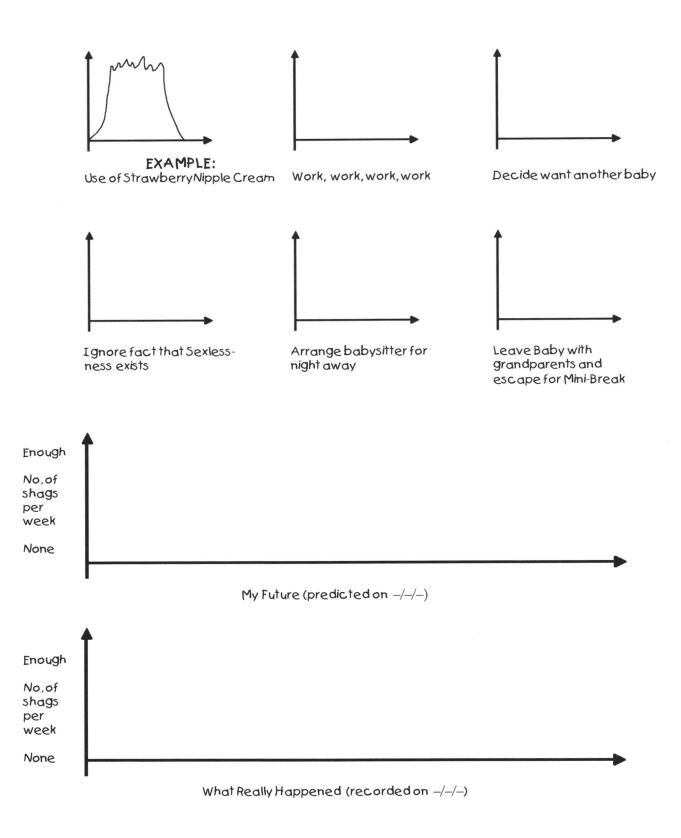

EXAMPLE:
Use of Strawberry Nipple Cream

Work, work, work, work

Decide want another baby

I ignore fact that Sexless-ness exists

Arrange babysitter for night away

Leave Baby with grandparents and escape for Mini-Break

Enough

No. of shags per week

None

My Future (predicted on –/–/–)

Enough

No. of shags per week

None

What Really Happened (recorded on –/–/–)

My Attitude to Sexlessness

It is important not to accept Sexlessness as a status quo!
Use the following table to monitor your attitude towards
Sexlessness - to check you're making progress.
(And go on, be honest!)

'I want sex* more than ...'

	Date	Date	Date	Date	Date
(tick box if yes)					
plateful of favourite pudding	❑	❑	❑	❑	❑
visit to Beauty Salon and Health Spa	❑	❑	❑	❑	❑
an extra 30 minutes of sleep	❑	❑	❑	❑	❑
an hour in front of favourite TV programme	❑	❑	❑	❑	❑
a long bath with bubbles and smelly candles	❑	❑	❑	❑	❑
trip to shops alone with NO baby buggy!	❑	❑	❑	❑	❑
session in café or bar with girlfriends	❑	❑	❑	❑	❑
romantic meal with partner	❑	❑	❑	❑	❑
30 minutes alone to do whatever I fancy	❑	❑	❑	❑	❑
other	❑	❑	❑	❑	❑
other...................................	❑	❑	❑	❑	❑
other...................................	❑	❑	❑	❑	❑
other...................................	❑	❑	❑	❑	❑

totals:

❑	❑	❑	❑	❑

* NB. sex referred to must be with
your regular partner

Your Score?

11 - 13	Brilliant! You're a Sex Goddess!
6-10	Not bad at all, Go Babe Go!
1-5	Congratulations! You are Ms Average
0	Oh dear ... attend therapy at once

Twenty Reasons Why I'm No Longer A Minxy Sex Kitten

If you don't feel horny, don't beat yourself up over it! Our survey of New Mothers showed that 96% of respondants have lost all interest in sex. If you're feeling sad, robbed or guilty at the sudden *migration* of your hormones (we believe they go to Ibiza where they are enjoyed by young trollopy women who haven't had babies yet), remind yourself that *it's just a passing phase.*

Justify your Sexlessness by completing the following list.
(Maybe leave it open on the pillow for your partner to read ...)

A Reminder to Myself
'I no longer feel like a Minxy Sex Kitten because ...'

1. The mere sight of a willy still reminds me of contractions.
2. SEX STILL HURTS!
3. I still can't even see the region south of my bulging belly, so how am I meant to get it turned on again?
4. I'm fat and my body wobbles in places it never has before.
5. Actually, because my hormones are an unruly bunch, I just *don't feel like it.*
6. I'm too bloody tired, dammit!
7. I'm wearing grey maternity bras and iron laced girdle knickers - you work it out!
8. ....
9. ....
10. ....
11. ....
12. ....
13. ....
14. ....
15. ....
16. ....
17. ....
18. ....
19. ....
20. ....

Your Minxy Sex Kitten Action Plan

The problem with reclaiming your Minxy Sex Kitten-ness is:
1) it takes time, and 2) it takes money. Sadly, New Mums normally have very little of either. But don't despair! Plan your revival here ...

Step One: Stop Spending Your Spare Cash on the Flippin' Baby!

(Each segment = £10, colour in relevant amount on each graph)

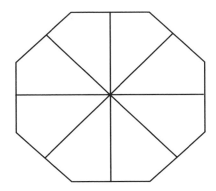

Graph 1
Proportion of my spare cash I spent on Baby this week.

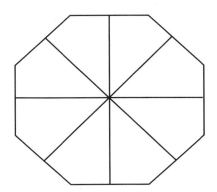

Graph 2
Proportion of my spare cash I spent on me this week.

The secret to success? Stop popping into The Early Learning Centre and buying stuff your baby *doesn't need*, and make yourself a Minxy Sex Kitten Shopping list instead...

Step Two: My Minxy Sex Kitten Shopping List

(Tick when purchased = mission accomplished!)

❑ sexy lingerie

❑ exercise video (for use, not decoration of TV shelf)

❑ new vibrator (sssssshhhh!!)

❑ new groovy make-up

❑ Stomach Reducing - Bust Lifting Super Dooper Waste of Money Cream, that will nevertheless do wonders for your mental wellbeing

❑ new pair of jeans that actually *fit properly* (regardless of size)

❑ a couple of bodice-ripping, lustful, romantic novels (to get you in the mood)

❑ cardboard cut-out of George Clooney or similar (anything's worth a try)

Ideas for other Minxy Sex Kitten stuff to buy, when more time and money arrives:

❑ ....

❑ ....

The Sex Token Game

Another irony of Sexlessness is the cruel fact that you and your partner will rarely, if ever, muster the energy and horniness for sex at the same time. Try to make light of this infuriating probability by playing our Sex Token Game. Because if you're both going to demand or deny sex occasionally (and annoy your partner immensely by doing so), some rules of play might help to keep things fair ...

The Rules

1. Each partner can play a maximum of *two* Sex Tokens and *two* Sleep Tokens each week.
2. How to play: when horny, place your Sex Token face up on your partner's pillow.
3. If your partner agrees with your indicated mood, abandon game and commence the fun.
4. If your partner disagrees with your indicated mood, they can void your request by playing a Sleep Token, should they have one left to play that week. Should they have no Sleep Tokens left, they must roll over, get ready, and chant 'it's for the good of my relationship' for as long as necessary.

- ✂ -

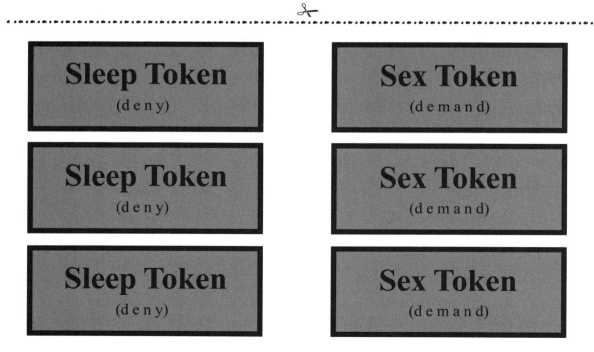

Maybe We Should Talk About It?

What's your partner thinking? Does he know what you're thinking?
We dare you to fill in the empty Thought Bubbles together ...

Mum's Progress Record No. 1

Date: Weight: Waist: Hips:

Diet & Exercise This Week:
Gold Star Award For:
Hopeless Cow Award For:

Coping With Being a New Mum:
Best Success This Week:

....

Worst Moment This Week:

....

Notes for Baby:
What I Love Most About You This Week

....

Things I Bought You This Week

....

Names I Called You This Week

....

Notes for Father:
The Loveliest Thing You Did This Week

....

The Most ANNOYING Thing You Did This Week

....

I Think I Might Have Annoyed You This Week When

....

Latest Top Tip (for the next baby)

....

Mum's Progress Record No.2

Date: Weight: Waist: Hips:

Diet & Exercise This Week:
Gold Star Award For:
Hopeless Cow Award For:

Coping With Being a New Mum:
Best Success This Week:

....

Worst Moment This Week:

....

Notes for Baby:
What I Love Most About You This Week

....

Things I Bought You This Week

....

Names I Called You This Week

....

Notes for Father:
The Loveliest Thing You Did This Week

....

The Most ANNOYING Thing You Did This Week

....

I Think I Might Have Annoyed You This Week When

....

Latest Top Tip (for the next baby)

....

Mum's Progress Record No. 3

Date: Weight: Waist: Hips:

Diet & Exercise This Week:
Gold Star Award For:
Hopeless Cow Award For:

Coping With Being a New Mum:
Best Success This Week:
....

Worst Moment This Week:
....

Notes for Baby:
What I Love Most About You This Week
....

Things I Bought You This Week
....

Names I Called You This Week
....

Notes for Father:
The Loveliest Thing You Did This Week
....

The Most ANNOYING Thing You Did This Week
....

I Think I Might Have Annoyed You This Week When
....

Latest Top Tip (for the next baby)
....

Mum's Progress Record No.4

Date: Weight: Waist: Hips:

Diet & Exercise This Week:
Gold Star Award For:
Hopeless Cow Award For:

Coping With Being a New Mum:
Best Success This Week:

....

Worst Moment This Week:

....

Notes for Baby:
What I Love Most About You This Week

....

Things I Bought You This Week

....

Names I Called You This Week

....

Notes for Father:
The Loveliest Thing You Did This Week

....

The Most ANNOYING Thing You Did This Week

....

I Think I Might Have Annoyed You This Week When

....

Latest Top Tip (for the next baby)

....

Mum's Progress Record No.5

Date: Weight: Waist: Hips:

Diet & Exercise This Week:
Gold Star Award For:
Hopeless Cow Award For:

Coping With Being a New Mum:
Best Success This Week:

....

Worst Moment This Week:

....

Notes for Baby:
What I Love Most About You This Week

....

Things I Bought You This Week

....

Names I Called You This Week

....

Notes for Father:
The Loveliest Thing You Did This Week

....

The Most ANNOYING Thing You Did This Week

....

I Think I Might Have Annoyed You This Week When

....

Latest Top Tip (for the next baby)

....

Mum's Progress Record No.6

Date: Weight: Waist: Hips:

Diet & Exercise This Week:

Gold Star Award For:

Hopeless Cow Award For:

Coping With Being a New Mum:

Best Success This Week:

....

Worst Moment This Week:

....

Notes for Baby:

What I Love Most About You This Week

....

Things I Bought You This Week

....

Names I Called You This Week

....

Notes for Father:

The Loveliest Thing You Did This Week

....

The Most ANNOYING Thing You Did This Week

....

I Think I Might Have Annoyed You This Week When

....

Latest Top Tip (for the next baby)

....

Mum's Progress Record No. 7

Date: Weight: Waist: Hips:

Diet & Exercise This Week:
Gold Star Award For:
Hopeless Cow Award For:

Coping With Being a New Mum:
Best Success This Week:

....

Worst Moment This Week:

....

Notes for Baby:
What I Love Most About You This Week

....

Things I Bought You This Week

....

Names I Called You This Week

....

Notes for Father:
The Loveliest Thing You Did This Week

....

The Most ANNOYING Thing You Did This Week

....

I Think I Might Have Annoyed You This Week When

....

Latest Top Tip (for the next baby)

....

Mum's Progress Record No. 8

Date: Weight: Waist: Hips:

Diet & Exercise This Week:
Gold Star Award For:
Hopeless Cow Award For:

Coping With Being a New Mum:
Best Success This Week:

....

Worst Moment This Week:

....

Notes for Baby:
What I Love Most About You This Week

....

Things I Bought You This Week

....

Names I Called You This Week

....

Notes for Father:
The Loveliest Thing You Did This Week

....

The Most ANNOYING Thing You Did This Week

....

I Think I Might Have Annoyed You This Week When

....

Latest Top Tip (for the next baby)

....

Mum's Progress Record No. 9

Date: Weight: Waist: Hips:

Diet & Exercise This Week:

Gold Star Award For:

Hopeless Cow Award For:

Coping With Being a New Mum:

Best Success This Week:

....

Worst Moment This Week:

....

Notes for Baby:

What I Love Most About You This Week

....

Things I Bought You This Week

....

Names I Called You This Week

....

Notes for Father:

The Loveliest Thing You Did This Week

....

The Most ANNOYING Thing You Did This Week

....

I Think I Might Have Annoyed You This Week When

....

Latest Top Tip (for the next baby)

....

Mum's Progress Record No. 10

Date: Weight: Waist: Hips:

Diet & Exercise This Week:
Gold Star Award For:
Hopeless Cow Award For:

Coping With Being a New Mum:
Best Success This Week:

....

Worst Moment This Week:

....

Notes for Baby:
What I Love Most About You This Week

....

Things I Bought You This Week

....

Names I Called You This Week

....

Notes for Father:
The Loveliest Thing You Did This Week

....

The Most ANNOYING Thing You Did This Week

....

I Think I Might Have Annoyed You This Week When

....

Latest Top Tip (for the next baby)

....

www.summersdale.com